Copyright © 2025 Different Reasons Inc.

All Rights Reserved.

Unauthorized use, reproduction, dissemination, or modification of any portion of this intellectual property is strictly, expressly and unequivocally prohibited. Violators shall be subject to immediate legal action, including but not limited to civil penalties, injunctive relief, under all applicable federal, state, and local laws. All material herein—explicitly including references to any individuals, families, businesses, organizations, or communities—is safeguarded by intellectual property laws and privacy protections. Any attempt to reprint, infringe, defame, misappropriate, or repurpose this content, whether by a licensee or an external party, constitutes a material breach and will be prosecuted to the maximum extent allowed by law. Written authorization from the appointed officers of Different Reasons Inc. is required for any resale, private, public, or commercial use, or redistribution.

ISBN: 979-8-218-68872-1 (Paperback)

ISBN: 979-8-218-68987-2 (Ebook)

LCCN: 2025910540

Publisher Information:

Different Reasons Inc.

Franklin, Tennessee

publishing@dreasons.com

Cover Design Inspired by The Richardson Legacy®

Different Reasons, Inc.

Journey Ready

The Legacy Experience®

Prelude

A

Love Story told by

Dr. DeAngelo Richardson

Our Prayer

Father, creator of all heaven and earth,

thank you for this glorious day that you have given us.

Thank you for your love, forgiveness, salvation, grace, and mercy that are set before us this day, that we continue to ask of you, so that we may experience the fullness of your holy glory for our lives.

Lord we ask that you continue to lead us into the fullness of your glory in spirit and in truth, that our lives may be fulfilled according to your will, purpose, and glory.

Cover our body, mind, heart, spirit, and soul, that we may walk humbly in your will, so that you may receive the glory for who we are, all the days of our life.

You are worthy to be praised, and we thank you for creating us to give you all the glory, honor, and praise, worshipping you as our eternal father, whom we call

Adonai, Elohim, Yahweh, Yeshua, Jehovah, Christ, Jesus, our victory banner, El Shaddai, and all that agreed said,

Amen.

Table of Contents

Our Prayer………..………………………….......……..4

A Message to My Beautiful Wife………...…..…….....7

Reader Disclaimer……………………………….…...8

Preface……………………………………….…...10

A Messages from The Doctor..…….....………….…...11

Special Thanks……………………………….…......17

Wisdom…………………………….......…......18

Marriage Wisdom…………………...…..……….19

A Covering of Love & Forgiveness…….................……23

And He Found His Holy Matrimony……....…..….…25

Journey Ready…………….…..………….......27

Different Reasons…..……………………..……28

And The Holy Spirit Reminded Him…….....…..…..40

Closing Words of Wisdom..42

Marital Lessons on Communication...........................44

Divine Revelation..46

Wisdom of The Temple..48

Acknowledgements..53

Yes, you don't see the word "Chapter" as a heading because everyone else does it. In a world where we can be different, be different, for Different Reasons.

The contents of this book are the giving of wisdom, knowledge, and understanding, as a result and reflection of the power of love, to minister the reconciliation of the heart and love of Christ. Always take yourself and your marriage before God as a holy and righteous covenant, for his glory.

A Letter to My Beautiful Wife

I give God the glory for our marriage and the beauty of life that I share with you. It's not the things we can do with time, or the things we have. It is one thing that I so very much cherish. It is that I have the love of God, and that it I share it with you. I want you to know that as long as we live and walk this life together, I will stand on the word of God for our marriage, allowing God to use me to break every chain and generational curse that is set before us. I will never let you go, and I will always stand before God on behalf of you and our children. I know that for myself, for you, and with you, with the fullness of love I have for myself, I have found the love of God. When I think about God, I think about you. When I think about you, the thought of you sends me back to God. It is the love I always wanted to experience in my life. What is this love that I speak of you may ask. The love of a holy matrimony. A life as a son of God. A life of love with you, with God as the foundation and Christ as the covering. Here is what I always want you to know, all the days of our lives together. This life I live for God, is all about God. For and with God, my life is now and will always be, all about you, and I, and our easy to satisfy children. You sometimes wonder if you're giving me what I want. God has already provided what I want and need. In the event you need a reminder, ask me, and I'll both tell and show you.

Until the end of time, I will hold you, love you, support you, and cover you in prayer, as my one and only WIFE.

Reader Disclaimer

This book is not written or to be read as a novel or story told in self-righteousness, or in vanity; as lustful desire for and of the eye, lustful desire for and of the flesh, or in the pride of life, but written and told in spirit and truth. This book is not constructed, written, or intended to lead readers and listeners to coveting or idolatry, and should stand only as a testimony of the power of love leading people and marriages back to God. Each reader or listener should examine himself or herself and seek God first for self-examination before, during, and after the reading or listening of this book or any other licensed and or published content associated with it before, during, or thereafter.

This book may be subject to revision by the author and publisher to maintain the fullness of truth, knowledge, wisdom, and understanding of God, warranting all readers and listeners of any version of this book to prayer for their own life, marriage, and salvation, to not model their lives after the people, characters, creators, publishers, or representatives of this book. All readers and listeners are advised to examine their hearts according to the first 10 mosaic laws, as well as the laws of Christ, written in the Holy Bible.

The authors, contributors, publisher, sponsors, and writers of this book are not responsible for any offense taken as a result of the reading, hearing, translation, or interpretation of the intent of the words written in this book, in dialogue, tone, tune, frequency, voice, language, grammar, spelling, coherency, or comprehension. or rhetoric but not limited to any of the aforementioned. Should any reader and listener of this book or any other copyright or licensed version or continuance of this book be offended by the stories or the content of this book and any book thereafter, we pray that you receive the love and revelation of the intent of this book, as it is not to be used as a tool of accusation or assumption, condemnation, devious entrapment, execution, extortion, idolization (idolatry), persecution, prosecution, restitution, or vengeance.

Turn to God in humility and prayer prior to reading this book the pages of this book. This book is to be read as one scroll of wisdom, knowledge, understanding, and revelation. Read each page of this book to receive the blessing it is indeed intended to be for your life in your preparation for marriage, or the marriage you are currently in. Consider the contents of this book as counsel to examine and edify yourself and to be reconciled to God for your own life, marriage, legacy of remembrance. This book is a story, not a standard. We are the body of Christ, and God is watching us all from the inside of our bodies.

Preface

This is a story that is being told, as "The Greatest In-Love Story Ever Told in Holy Matrimony." This story did not surface without the of the experiences of life, but through the desire of a man and woman to live their life according to the ways of God, giving glory, honor, praise, and worship to God in spirit and truth. The heart of the story is about a man who consistently sought the will of the father for his life and his marriage, to fully submit himself to the will of God by obeying God's voice. The man of God would grow to develop his own personal relationship with God, by continuously living in all effort to be the word of God and not just speak it. He too, would live to display a life that would lead people back to God through love, forgiveness, grace, and mercy, to receive salvation, revival, restoration, and redemption as a servant of the kingdom of God. Giving thanks for love, salvation, forgiveness, grace, and mercy, He would honor God in his life, with his marriage. This book is solely, about the love of God and the love a man freely shared, with his wife and children, in holy matrimony, so that they could display to the world, the beauty of God and family.

Disclaimer: Marriage is a sacred union and covenant between God, man, and woman, and shall not be infringed upon by any person. If you seek a husband or wife, seek God first, with your body, mind, heart, spirit, and soul.
Its a covenant agreement, not a contract agreement.

A Message from The Doctor

The only way to experience life, is to experience life the way God desires for us all. It is not different from the way he originally intended in the beginning. The greatest mistake we make in life is desiring a life that appears to be greater than the life that God has given us. What he has of us is not the life that we want or the life that we forcefully try to produce ourselves. If we listen close enough, he will speak what he wants for us to desire to fulfill his will for our life. The word says that he will give us the desires of our heart. It is to say, that he will give us what he wants our hearts to desire, because what he desires for us is for him to get the glory. We must stop resisting the will of God. Understand that we cannot outwork or our run the will of God. We will tire ourselves out, going nowhere, as fast and far as we can, by living our lives in fear or self-righteousness.

Husbands, Love God first, and he will teach you how he wants you to love yourself, then how to love your wife (his daughter). Wives, love God first, and he will teach you how to love yourself, first, then how to love your husband (his son). We are the first example of love that our children will see. Because we are not always perfect, we must always seek God, so that our children know that even when we stumble, just as they will, God is there to pick us up. Husbands, never leave your wife. Wives, never leave your husband. Look for new things to love about one another. God is renewing us daily, so there is always something new to see in your loving spouse. Live your lives in the fruit of the spirit, so that you can walk this journey of life together. Keep your covenant with God and your spouse.

Keep in mind, at all times, that we are spirits dwelling inside of a body. In a marriage, you are not only one flesh with your spouse, but one spirit also. The flesh is only a reflection of what you are seeing and experiencing of yourself or the generational curses (trauma) of one another's bloodline and family lineage. It is not for you to take offense, but to help you understand what God is asking you to pray for, but also how to practice grace. If you are seeing something unpleasant in your spouse, it is either a reflection of you, or something they need your help being delivered from through prayer, fasting, and patience. Do not assume that your spouse knows how you feel or what you are experiencing. It is your responsibility to diligently and peacefully explain it to them in a way that they understand. While one spirit, you too, are still two completely different vessels, walking in effort to help one another understand God, life, and one another. Do not fear one another, but also do not provoke one another, as the problems of life are already excessive.

Men

The best love you can give your wife is a pure unadulterated love, which is the love of Christ. That love is, to give them a love that they do not deserve. That is the type of love that minsters to their hearts that you truly love them.

It should never warrant them to take advantage of you, or you to take advantage of them. When love is true and unadulterated it will find every effort to show, and they will see it. It is not just words, thoughts, or actions. It is a love that shows them that you will never give up on them. The way to do that is to always seek the father for what she needs. Her body and mind are always changing because of the experiences of life but also because of her hormones, especially after childbirth, but also as a result of the influences of the world that leads her to coveting, or idolatry, as with Eve in the garden. Be patient during postpartum. She is healing. Be a man of God, servant of Christ, and a keeper of the holy spirit for that woman that you have a covenant with. God honors covenants that you make with him in spirit and truth, but most importantly, what gives him the glory. Get to know your wife. All women are not the same, though the same in nature. Do not expect perfection.

Women

Be mindful that your husband is already under the pressures of spiritual and natural warfare of releasing his body, mind, heart, spirit, and even soul from the ways of the world that entrapped him into believing that money, sex, power, respect, pride, success, and gluttony is what he should desire. Help to bring him peace and adequate rest so that he may continue to hear from God and what the father's will is for the life of the family. Ask him what he wants/needs. What he wants is what will keep him moving, trusting your support. As a man of God, there is a strong possibility that all he wants is, Love, Order,

Respect, Understanding, Sex (but in pleasant moderation), Submission, Loyalty, and Prayer. These 8 things are what keeps him feeling secure, so that you may feel secure as well. He will freely provide, protect, and serve. Give every effort to take stress off of his mind. Examine yourself so that you do not bring him hurt, heartbreak, or disappointment. He already wants to give you himself over to you. Do not lie to or manipulate him. If he is a praying man, he already knows the truth. He also is not in competition with other men. Daily, he is at war within himself, fighting the influences of the battlefield of his body, mind, heart, and spirit, to protect his soul from any tie of enemies of God. Daily, he is becoming a servant of God's Kingdom, but a vessel for you. Get to know your husband. All men are not the same, though the same in nature. Do not expect perfection.

Always love, because it is the purest thing you can do. Forgive, because there will come a time, where you will want and need it as well. Never judge one another. Never abandon one another. Remember that in marriage, you are one. To do to your spouse, is to do to yourself (this applies to the husband and the wife). Do not waste time searching for problems, for the problems of life are already many. Never fight over resources. It's not yours anyway. Help keep the love of God in the center of your lives, as well as your marriage. God bless you those who receive this message. My prayer is that God washes away your sins, so that you too, can be free from your past, because you deserve it. Yesterday does not exist; only your memory of it does. Do not hold on to the past, as it is already gone. As Christ would say, "Sin no more".

" I was sitting in my living room one day and I heard God tell me that he wants me to give him the glory for everything. I sat up and said to myself to him that its an easy ask, but my next question in response to him was how. I sat down for days wondering what he would tell me to do, and he told me to start this book series. Ironically, this was 4-5 months after I told my therapist that my marriage would known as the greatest love story ever told. Months later, it was apart of the book title, highlighting the beginning of the bok series. One of her questions to me that I'll ever forget was *"When you die, what do you want to be remembered for?"* I told her:

"I want to be remembered for my love for God. Nothing else matters."

I let the spirit guide me into every step of this entire book series and God has not stopped blessing me since. I found out that a lot of people who said or made me feel as though they actually loved me, only loved me for what I could give, who I could be for them, or what I could do for them, never for who I am. Very interesting experience. Many say that they love God until its time to show it."

Special Thanks

There are many people who can receive thanks for the development of this book. This book, however, is written from the experiences of life, but also as a result of communion and personal relationship with God in the journey of life. There is only one way to properly give thanks for the creation, production, and publication of this book. That is, to thank the one person who deserves it the most and alone. He is the creator of all people, places, and things. He is then, now, and to come. He is above, inward, beneath, and roundabout. He is darkness and light. He is eternal. He is God.

"THANK YOU GOD, FOR EVERYTHING."

Wisdom

Do not take a second in life for granted or people and the time that you have with them in life. Love what God has given you, because someone in the world does not have what you have. Take nothing for granted. If there is something or someone in life that you are without, it is because it or they are not yours, or you have made it an idol, placing it or their importance in your life before the importance of God.

Marriage Wisdom

1.) Never replace God with anything to take the place of what he can do in your life & marriage. Anything else that is in and of the world will not fix you, your spouse, or your marriage. Only God can, when you allow him to. Keep him first in all things as a family.

2.) Never do or say anything to make your spouse think, feel, say, or believe that you no longer want, need, desire, or love them. They are to be accepted and cherished by you, not rejected by you. Never let your CHILDREN or PARENTS come in between your marriage, or anyone/anything else.

3.) Never use your spouse for your own selfish desires. What God has given you is for you to share with one another to build each other up, not tear each other down. It's what your children need to see so that they may desire a righteous way of living in their marriage as well.

4.) Keep your family, friends, and/or anyone else in the world out of the marital concerns or issues of your marriage. Their desire to see you "happy" is out of their allegiance to who they want you to be and not who God needs you to be for his purpose and will. Hearkening to their voice is also Idolatry. Only God knows what YOU are to do. It is, to seek him for healing and understanding in those moments.

5.) A marriage should never have boundaries between spouses. The only boundaries that should exist are the boundaries of what to keep away from your marriage, home and children. Your home is your sanctuary, your marriage is your covenant seal, and you should not allow any and everyone into it unwarrantedly and unrighteously. That includes your birth family. Consider that boundaries are barriers as places in your life, marriage, and home as areas of life that need both transformation and healing.

6.) Pour into each other and your home first before you do or give anything away to anyone else. If anyone desires anything of you as someone who is not a part of your home and family, if there is not an agreement between you and your spouse, it should never happen.

7.) Keep the 10 (really 11 that makes it 1) commandments of God and the fullness thereof. In all of them, flows the inheritance of the Kingdom of Heaven.

8.) Do not provoke your spouse into sin as a result of your lack of patience or relationship, or obedience to God. If God is building your spouse in a way that does not look familiar to you, it is for his will and not yours.

9.) Never deceive your spouse. God reveals all.

10.) Never stop praying with and for one another, as prayer is a great submission to God, but also one of the greatest acts of love.

11.) Always remember that you and your spouse are one with each other, and one with God.

12.) The last is this which is extremely overlooked and undermined. When it comes to your spouse, speak life into them, and speak the beauty of life about them. Be a representation of honor to and for them in spite of all differences. Marriage is refinement, not perfection.

A Covering of Love and Forgiveness

Father who created all heaven and earth, we forgive any and everyone who has sinned against you, our God, in effort or attempt, knowingly or unknowingly, willingly or unwillingly, by but not limited to act, order, conspiracy, accusation, or judgement to bring our family, or any other person, community, or organization for any of, but not limited to hurt, harm, danger, sorrow, pain, loss, grief, or oppression, with words, thoughts, actions, emotions, beliefs, or alliances. We pray the love and blood of Christ over the readers and hearers of his prayer and the lives of their bloodline, living and unborn, to save us from the ways of the world that are unholy & a continuation of generational sin, unrighteousness, and divisiveness, of us, our families, and livelihoods & charity. Set us free to live our lives this moment forward without sin.

God we ask and pray that you watch over us internally and externally to protect us as well from any hurt, harm, danger, sorrow, loss, or grief, with words, thoughts, actions, emotions, beliefs, or alliances set before us from this moment on forward. We pray the reconciliation of our life to you God, through Christ. As we believe in your heart and confess with our mouths through faith that Jesus is lord who died for the remission of our sins; to lead, guide, and direct us to a life of love, in spirit and in truth, as the salt and light of the world. Thank you for the salvation of the world lord, that the confession for us all, is that all living things in the heavens above, in the earth beneath, in the waters thereof, or anything beneath, are nothing without you. Thank you for everything, Eternal Living Father, creator of all.

Adonai, Elohim, Yahweh, Yeshua, Christ, Jehovah, Jesus

El Shaddai

You are, that you are.

"God is who he is to me, and every name I call him is a result of him showing me evidence of who he is by acknowledging him that way."

(This prayer is a shared prayer for those who want and/or need words to speak to the father, should you not be able to find them yourself as a gift of grace).

And He Found His Holy Matrimony

This is the beginning of a story about how one of the world's most loving couples came together at the beginning of their love journey that began at a winery. They were two individuals from the Midwest, who grew up in broken homes, experiencing a life of trauma, abuse, violence, neglect, abandonment, as well as the greatest pain of all, a loss of a love. As a result of this unhealthy childhood, they each navigated through life living with the guidance and preparation of their elders and the like-minded individuals in their lives that understood the divinity of who they were. While they did not grow up in the same town, they were born in the same year, just under 30 days apart, less than 200 miles away from one another.

A distinguishing discovery of this revelation, is that they were called and chosen to be born a with heart condition that they would both share together, eventually leading them both to experiencing a myriad of ups and downs, and heartbreak & rejection from others that would eventually bring them together. Their toughest battle individually (and what would someday be collectively) was being able to discover who they were individually, and sometimes, who they were becoming together. Prior to them crossing paths, they both would live a life experiencing the victimization of generational sins as a result of poor leadership from their peers, leaders, guardians, and unfortunately, their birth families. They would spend life, breaking chains of spiritual bondage and unwanted soul ties together.

Journey Ready

As they Journey through life, living and seeking clarity and understanding as to why they had experienced so much despair, turmoil, and grief, they would also experience a great deal of remorse as a result of a lack of wisdom, knowledge and understanding of how they're unhealed hearts caused them to hurt others and sometimes, one another because of their commitment to God. At some point in time in their lives before they met, they both sought God in prayer alone, which ultimately led them to a common location where they would both be discovered by one another, both wearing a distinct combination of colors that would be the first sign from God.

Different Reasons Inc.

In a very special year, where light would begin to shine to and through them both, A man in search of the love of God, was standing outdoors as she began to walk by him, confirming something that was for his eyes only. It was without doubt, that God had finally began to align them both in time of what would become a covenant in sacred holy matrimony in the coming years. During this journey, their first date took place in a room full of roses and music, where he enjoyed the simplicity of their conversation. They experienced their first date at what is believed to be a Jamaican diner where they would enjoy their two favorite entrees. They would later enjoy a very relaxing date at a vineyard & winery, where they both would enjoy what would become their favorite bottle of wine together to embrace the unleashing of their love for one another. Following this date, they went to play golf, a hobby that would become one of their family's favorite quality time moments of recreation.

Though they would go on to experience hardship together, they would never neglect the responsibility of praying for one another, despite their breach in communication. Through prayer, they would both only want one another to live their lives in the will of God, where he would get the glory for not just their lives individually, but their marriage as well. What is most interesting, is that no matter how difficult it was for them both to continue to grow and develop, they would always seek to be more of what they wanted from the other, which was to be more like Christ, and loved by one another. The core element to what binds them both, is that they never stop trying to be who God expects them to be, for his glory, and not their own, for his will and not their own desires.

One of the most inspiring moments of their story, is that the winery where they had their first date of relaxation, it would go on to inspire them to love and create together, an initiative led by the Husband and Father of their family. They made beautiful children and created a family that reflects and displays love, though struggling with disagreements like all marriages. The most important discovery of this collective union is that the Husband would eventually agree to trust that his entire family believed in Christ, as they confessed it together as a family on New Years Eve during the year of one of their special anniversaries, though all of them are special. What would go on to happen, is that the husband would fall asleep and wake up rested, feeling thankful in faith that he had done what he believe was in his heart, which was to give himself & his family back to God.

As a family, they would be known to create beautiful moments together, which continued to inspire the husband and father to continue to create other things and ideas to help make the world a better place, with the help and prayers of his wife and children. One of their most inspiring creations, was the selling of their own family wine glasses and coffee mugs that highlights the beginning of their love journey but also to help tell the story of how special they are as a family to raise the money needed to build schools for children, and support families in need. During times of relaxation, the husband would sip his favorite wine with joy as he reflects on how God can heal his body, free his mind, clean his heart, renew his spirit, and save & bless his soul. In doing so, he would desire for God to bless him to be a blessing to and for his wife, through obedience of the spoken word of God, given to him as a gift, reward, and blessing of his own personal relationship with God, in spirit and in truth. He then, would work with his wife to be a blessing to others, led by the holy spirit.

As they continue to experience their journey of life, through the challenges and experiences that continued to equip them for their divine journey, they would experience a life of fulfillment of love through Christ and the fruit of the spirit, which are love, faithfulness, peace, joy, kindness, goodness, gentleness, patience, and self-control. In those, they would find prosperity in the simplicity of life as a family and would freely travel the world as a display of the power of love as a ministry of divine joy. Though imperfectly perfect, they would become the perfect gem of life and light as a display of the power of true love, and a testimony of the experience of children of God, and teachers of love and life.

In contentment of the blessings of faith, truth, and divine revelation, the husband would often dwell in his favorite secret place, to repent and pray to God, so that he may hear from God freely to keep himself from sinning. He would then, pray with his heart of forgiveness, for those who have committed sin, in ways that brought him pain, hurt, harm, danger, loss, grief, or confusion. While sitting in his favorite place for prayer and relaxation, after his visitations from God, he would enjoy his favorite beverage to drink with his wife, being grateful for his life, where he lives a life of unadulterated love, in the fullness of his love for God and the family God gave him a covenant with. He would often look at his glass water after a few sips to find the one thing that always reminds him of God, his wife, his family, and himself. It was and will always be his commitment to his covenant of holy matrimony. God would then tell him one day in a small still voice, that he was well pleased, making his family Journey Ready™ for Different Reasons™. His covenant with God was to obey God by living his life through faith, and to have his lovely and beautiful wife, for good or bad, through sickness and health, for rich or for poor, all the days of his life.

Because of his love and zeal for God, he would commit with his whole heart to God, and his wife and children. The husband would often seek alone time to hear from God, to be able to continuously give God glory, honor, and praise. He would worship openly, and sometimes even shout loudly with the fullness of breath and life in him, unashamed, to express his never-ending love for God. He would often reflect on the humor of God and how he tells him the story of how and why he brought him and his wife together, giving him memories of moments in time where he would use people, places, and things to keep his mind and heart focused on God's will for his life, and also the reason he was doing it. It would all be, for his wife and children, but mostly, for his glory. Each day that had gone by, he would be in continuous preparation for what would be not just the woman of his heart's desire, but the woman of God that was made perfect for him.

Two statements made in life by the husband and wife about one another in a most humble display of humility to God.

The Husband: "God, please send me MY WIFE."

The Wife: "I want MY HUSBAND."

Journey Ready

The wife would one day confess to her husband that she came to the divine revelation that God had already revealed to him in their bedroom after a very disappointing moment in time and a time of separation. It was one of many prophetic spoken words from God himself that he often kept a secret. It was that they were predestined to meet to be together as Husband and Wife.

As a family with all of their children, they confessed individually, and prayed together saying:

"We believe and confess that Jesus is Lord."

The Husband would continue grow, learn, and realize what life is all about, and gave his beautiful wife the most powerful and anointed sentence of words he as a man had ever given to a woman. It was a statement that he never wrote or spoke before in all the years of his life until this very moment she received the message. It was a moment and statement that God gave him to reveal the condition of his heart, to show her his true devotion to her. She received those words as a birthday gift on her 34th birthday with the visual proof of how God uses her husband to bless her as a result of his submission to God as a loving and faithful husband. The presentation included the statement:
"You are first in my life because God is first in my life."
Though it was a small gesture, to the husband, it meant everything to give to her as joyful proof of God's revelation of her divine identity through his gift of digital marketing & branding.

The husband fell so deeply in love with his wife as a result of his love for God, that he learned that God had answered one of his favorite prayers, which for God to help him become a better Husband and Father.

The prayer was so powerful, that it would come true every day, even when he did not speak the words verbally.

The wife would grow to learn that her loving and faithful husband devoted himself to God in such a way, that he and God would spend unlimited secret time together in communication about all the ways God would bless them and their children. Though God continued to reveal the blessings he had for him as a faithful servant, he only wanted to accept them, to share it with his wife and children in appreciation of an answered prayer, after an unforgettable experience that they had as husband and wife.

Honoring his covenant to God of what he wanted in life after the experience, God would go on to bless him, because he never asked God for money, fame, power, death to his enemies, or anything else that is of the world that would not bring God glory. His request was often speculated upon, as he and his family would travel the world to share the stories of the blessing of God and the power of righteous prayer. One of those requests, was for him to always be what his wife wanted, which was a man of God, as a husband of one wife, to give her the love that she deserved. That love is a love that he trusted God to never fade, fail, or falsify. He as a husband, would submit to God in such a way, that he did not know how to not love his wife.

AndThe Holy Spirit Reminded Him

While they were dating before they wed together, the wife, spoke her request to him in a way that he understood, though she did not understand the words she had just spoken. She said:

"I do not want anyone to have you the way that I have you."

What she did not know in that moment was that it would be the day that she spoke words from her mouth that only God could give her, to fulfill a prophecy to him about the knowledge, existence, and vision of his heaven-sent wife.
He as a man would begin to give more effort to separate himself from the ways of his carnal mind as well as his flesh, and the things in his life that so easily beset him from the presence of, and relationship with God himself.

The husband would go on to live his life, in all effort, obeying the voice of God according to their own personal relationship together, to continue to be a faithful servant, and a loving and faithful Husband of his one and only Beautiful Wife, and Father of their children, as the man of God of their family. The beautiful married couple would go on to be known as The Legacy Experience™, a beautiful story about the love of God in The Greatest In-Love Story Ever Told in Holy Matrimony.

It is a story and what would become one of the world's most exciting events in over 80 locations worldwide to help build communities, schools, support families, and a time to share the best stories that can ever be told stories of about the love of God and the sacredness of Marriage.

Closing Words of Wisdom

Men & women, if we refrain from satisfying our flesh and selfish desires, we will begin to see the opposite gender for who they are and not seeing them as objects or tools of usage. Seek God in your life's experiences, trusting the process of your journey of healing and discovery of identity. We assure you, that you will discover the root of why we as people cannot properly love. The answer will lead us all to something very simple. God wants us to seek him to find out for ourselves (others may guide you). He wants us all to experience his love first, so that we know how to properly love others, especially our spouses. Love can happen to and for all of us. Money cannot and will not buy the freedom of love that we are all looking for. It is given from God.
If a woman is not your wife, keep your body, mind, heart, spirit, and soul off of and away from her. If a man is not your husband, keep your body, mind, heart, spirit, and soul off of her. Disobeying this

instruction is breach of a sacred covenant that has consequences from God himself.
Lastly, do not look to find a spouse better than the one you have. If you're seeing something wrong in them it is because they reflect you. Do not abandon your responsibility to love them because they too, want and need the love that you desire as well. Do not be afraid or ashamed to be seen happily with them or speak openly that you are married. Do not denounce your marriage to fulfill the interest of yourself or others. Your spouse will be happy, as long as they are made to feel secure with you. Don't assume that they are (communicate). Allow God to get the glory for your life and marriage, because he can, and will, as a keeper of righteous and holy covenants.
Do not marry for the benefit of it. Marry for love. It always prevails.

Seek God with a **heart of repentance** for **forgiveness**. **Faith** is to **repentance** as **repentance** is to **obedience**, where **obedience**, is to **salvation**.

Marital Lessons of Communication

There is a myth that suggests that communication is key. While true to the vagueness of its context, it does not provide the clarity of understanding needed to be able to learn how to effectively communicate in a way that keeps couples together in understanding.

The first key to communication is choosing to not be afraid to diligently express yourself without seeking to offend your spouse. The second is to be a listening spouse that does not take offense to the words of your husband/wife. The third thing is to understand that it is important to properly communicate with words what you're trying to say about how you are feeling. Your words will help your spouse understand what you are experiencing. Your spouse can only understand what they are experiencing from you as a spirit inside their own body, just as you are. Usually, that is connecting with a part of them that they understand or don't.

The difficult thing to understand in communication, is that you are receiving what you are experiencing as a result of the reflection of your own internal spirit. You are either seeing the person you used to be, the person that you are holding on to (your old self), or the person that you are becoming. Take this as an opportunity to ask questions about what you are seeing for understanding, so that you can resolve the issues or rejoice. It will automatically communicate with through love, that you love the person you're in covenant relationship with as well. The law of communication simple but complicated because it is a process of development overtime as a result of learn or unlearned beliefs that become behaviors; behaviors that become lifestyles, and lifestyle that become identity. Identity is who you should become in Christ.

Divine Revelation

"When I chose to marry my wife, I did it because I knew God had sent not only what I prayed for, but what he had been preparing me for the entire time. When I made my vow, I made them to God first, then I made them to her. It took a lot of hard work for me to move from darkness to the light, but I never gave up and I never stopped looking within myself for things I wanted God to change about me, but also how to continue to do the best I can at being the husband she wanted and needed because it was something that was not taught to me or done in the 5 generations of men in my family that I know about. Because of my faithfulness to God first, he helped me to be faithful to my wife. When the fullness of faithfulness came to me, he did something that you'll read about in another book. One day he woke me up and told me about his will for my life. 24 hours later he confirmed it and told my wife, and she told me what she believes she heard him say. That was all the confirmation I needed to know about what God wanted from me and who he wanted me to experience this life with, because it would lead to us both doing something that we both love to do most together. There is so much more to this story. I'm only telling it because God told me to. I didn't make all the right decisions in life or marriage, and no one really does, but I never gave up on God and what he could do. I give him glory, that this book is one of my rewards for being a good and faithful servant for choosing to please God and not people. *LOVE* always wins."

Wisdom of the Temple

The Body

The body is a reflective function of who God designed us to be. It is a full explanation of how everything works and flows together. Its methods of communication bring awareness through the 5 senses of sight, smell, taste, hearing, and feeling. Whatever the body is experiencing is an awareness of a spiritual reality unseen, communicated naturally.

The Mind

The mind is the motor and memory unit of the body. It directs the body according to the body's wants, needs, or desires. The mind has to be properly trained and nurtured by things of God, edifying the wants, needs, and desires of the body, but also, so that the mind remains pure of the infirmities (sin) of life that sends the body into paths of unrighteousness. The condition of the mind will reveal to us how we're obeying or disobeying the voice and/or word of God.

The Heart

The heart is the where the flow of life is. How we tend to it through the mind and the body can determine the outcome of our natural and spiritual reality. Whatever we feed body and mind, we feed our heart's desires. It can be duplicitous, which is why giving it back to God is vital. The ways of the world twist the heart into deception, blindly. We should always examine our hearts to find if we are desiring things of the God or the enemies of God.

The Spirit

The spirit is the presence of either a clean or unclean roots. A clean and righteous spirit is the reflection of holy refinement of the body, mind, and heart. When it is un-clean, it reflects an unholy body, mind, and heart. What the body, mind, and heart are experiencing together in life, externally, shows us who we are as spirits internally. When the body, mind, and heart are polluted, the righteous spirit departs. When renewed and refreshed, it dwells and permeates. Our natural and spiritual experiences are a matter of us inviting or rejecting God.

The Soul

The soul is the eternal living of the body, mind, heart, and spirit, unseen in the fullness of who we are. Whatever our body, mind, heart, and spirit make agreements with determines the outcome of our soul's eternal dwelling. The heavenly or hell like experiences of life are a matter of what we submit to, mirroring our life beyond what we can see. Our choices of obeying and disobeying God direct the paths of the body, mind, heart, and spirit. Yes we have free will, but free will to either obey, or disobey. All of it is used narrow our walk with God in this journey of life, to dwell with him eternally the way he designed for us in the beginning prior to sin. The greatest obedience is to obey the laws of Christ, to receive salvation, revival, redemption, restoration, and reconciliation. Obey the law of Love (Love, forgives, grace, mercy, salvation) Love, is the epitome of spiritual fruit, and the fullness of the Glory of God.

Always remember, that you never have to live with your choices. God is watching everything we do from inside our bodies. God can always turn things around if it is in his will and his divine timing. That is why he is God.

When asked why the husband loves his wife so much, he replied:

"I don't know how not to. It's a love only God could teach me."

He later revealed that God visit him in a place full of midst, and asked him why God himself, hated divorce. He shared his answer:

" Because it has nothing to do with me and her. It has everything to do with your will and your glory."

He was then asked of what God wanted, He return God's spoken word to him, the words he spoke was:

"All of the Glory"

Then he said,

"In Jesus Name."

He gave more wisdom as a result of God's correction of ungodly wisdom given and shown to him as a man seeking a wife. It was, to marry for money. He would go on to marry his wife, for one reason and one reason only:

"Love, in spirit and in truth."

This breakout story is brought to you by The Legacy Experience™, with honorable mention and thanks to Dr. DeAngelo Richardson™, Journey Ready®, Divine Road®, Garden Rose® Season Ready®. Divine Joy®, Zentih Productions LLC, and Our Eternal living creator for their contribution to the discovery, revelation, and development of the book series. All content, designs, and images contained in this book are subject to licensing and copyright laws. Unauthorized use, copying, defamation, or distribution is strictly prohibited and may lead to legal action.

Acknowledgements

With esteemed honor and acknowledgement to the one and only person who deserves acknowledgement as a testimony of proof of the power, spirit, and truth of love in this book, who is, the creator of all heaven and earth, a creator called by the names known of the author to be:

Adonai, Elohim, Yahweh, Yeshua, Jehovah, Christ, Jesus.

God Almighty

El Shaddai

You are, that you are.

"Your marriage is the greatest marriage in holy matrimony. You just have to believe that it is and be willing to give God a marriage he can get the glory for. He deserves it. Secular and worldly concepts and practices will never work to sustain what is meant to be a spiritual relationship. If you dont want God involved in it, don't do it."

"Whoso findeth a wife findeth a good thing and obtaineth favor from the lord (Proverbs 18:22, KJV)."

"The wife is not the good thing. God's order is, and God's order restores innocence."

-Dr. DeAngelo Richardson

In loving honor and respect of The Beautiful Married Couple.

To get notified of the next release and follow the series, scan the QR code below:

Want to order more copies of this Prelude? Scan the QR code below:

ENJOYED THE READ? RECOMMEND IT TO A FRIEND, FAMILY MEMBER, OR ORGANIZATION.

www.ingramcontent.com/pod-product-compliance
Lightning Source LLC
Chambersburg PA
CBRC092029050526
44107CB00116B/1282/J